*An Insider's Guide
to Managing Your*

*Chronic
or
Terminal Illness*

Nancy A. Matthews

An Insider's Guide to Managing Your

Chronic or Terminal Illness

Nancy A. Matthews

© 2008 by Nancy A. Matthews

ISBN: 1440401152
EAN-13:   9781440401152

Cover photo by Vance Carruth

Published by CreateSpace
A DBA of On-Demand Publishing LLC
www.createspace.com

Website: www.nancyamatthews.com

Nancy Matthews
P.O. Box 5
Westons Mills, NY 14788
nancymatthews74@yahoo.com

I would like to dedicate this book to
Jeanne Smith

Jeanne, you gave me the confidence and
support I needed to believe in my own
ability to take control of my medical
situation and become the best
self-advocate I could be.

Contents

Acknowledgements

I would like to offer my deepest gratitude to:

My friends who are personally affected by chronic illness: Ashleigh Donner, Betty Lundburg, Cammi Stohl Brady, Julie Trahan, and Lara Govendo; thank you for your support, understanding, wonderful feedback, and willingness to assist me with this project.

My excellent editors: Ann and Vance Carruth, thank you for being here when I needed you; and Deb Bookmiller, your input has been invaluable.

The mental health professionals who reviewed this guide for its clinical relevance: Thomas Delaney, PhD; Ruth Palmquist, MSEd; Amy Lafler, MSEd; and Rose Ruffner, MSEd.

The medical professionals who evaluated the health care strategies outlined: Jill Delaney, RN; Pat Champion, RN; Jeff Szymanski, PA; Susan Lancelotta, MD; and Nick Koutrelakos, MD.

Dr. Witte, Dr. Pilewski, and Dr. Cronin; for trusting me to be an equal partner in my medical care.

The nurses and staff at UPMC, especially, Kelly Ohrman, Paul Moran Pillage, Deborah Piontek, and Maureen Emerling.

The nurses and staff at the Olean Medical Group for your excellent care!

The CF Care Team at WCHOB for your education, support, and friendship.

The nurses from the Cattaraugus County Health Department for their wonderful home care!

All of the nurses who have cared for me during my many hospitalizations; I believe God holds a special place in His heart for excellent nurses like you!

Introduction

If you have been recently diagnosed or are currently dealing with a chronic or terminal illness, this book was written for you. We may not know each other or have ever met, but I want to help you learn how to successfully manage your medical condition.

Through my own years of chronic illness, I have had to learn many of these lessons the hard way, through trial and error. Hopefully my experiences, and the strategies outlined, can serve as a guide to help you avoid the frustrations I have felt, and move you directly toward successful control over your medical situation.

Any time I start reading a book like this, I wonder what expertise the author has, so I would like to share a little of my background with you.

At the age of six I was diagnosed with cystic fibrosis (CF). For those of you who are unfamiliar with CF, it is a genetic disorder that affects the lungs and pancreas. Cells in the body produce thick, sticky mucus that clogs the tubes and passageways within the body.

This clogging prevents the pancreas from being able to produce the enzymes necessary for digestion, and, over time, causes scarring, inflammation, and infections in the lungs which can lead to respiratory failure and death (www.cff.org).

As a child, the major symptoms I experienced were digestive; my lung complications didn't really begin until my freshman year of college. At this time, I was diagnosed with a non-malignant brain tumor on my pituitary gland. The medications used to try to shrink the tumor caused my body to become vulnerable to infection. During Christmas break of my freshman year, I was hospitalized with pneumonia and sinusitis. My illness was so severe, I was not able to return to college for the second semester, but instead remained at home to have sinus surgery and, eventually, brain surgery to remove the tumor.

My return to college the following year was difficult. I started experiencing the effects of CF in a dramatic and traumatizing way. My lungs began to bleed excessively causing hemoptysis (coughing up blood). I was hospitalized with each new episode and spent over four weeks in the hospital during my sophomore year. My doctors finally realized this was part of my disease progression and could not be resolved through hospitalization.

In the years that followed, I had several medical set-backs and was hospitalized periodically for "tune-ups" (IV antibiotic treatments). I battled Aspergillus (a fungal lung infection); survived two spontaneous pneumothoraxes (collapsed lungs); dealt with numerous lung infections; developed diabetes; had my gall bladder removed and a feeding tube inserted into my stomach.

Despite my medical struggles, I completed my Master's Degree in counseling and worked in both clinical and career counseling settings.

In 1999, I discovered my true passion, counseling college students with medical, psychological, and learning disabilities and had the honor of serving as the Coordinator of Disability Support Services at St. Bonaventure University for seven and a half years.

In January of 2007, my body entered the end stages of CF, and I had to retire from my position at the University. Without a double lung transplant, my condition would be terminal and, based on my current lung functions, I was given approximately two more years to live.

I was fortunate to be accepted by the University of Pittsburgh Medical Center's Cardiopulmonary Transplant Program, one of two in the United States to accept high-risk cases like mine. I am currently listed and waiting for the miracle of new lungs that could extend my life a few more years.

I hope this brief overview helps you to understand how I gained my knowledge, experience, and expertise. May my experiences, both positive and negative, and the lessons I have learned from them, offer you the insight and information you need to successfully manage your condition.

I invite you to use this guide as a manual to assist you in becoming the best self-advocate you can be. Feel free to read it chapter by chapter, or jump around to the sections that will assist with your current situation. I hope the information you learn within its pages will help you as much as it has helped me.

CHAPTER ONE

Dealing with Your Diagnosis

Discovering you have a chronic illness or that a pre-existing condition has entered its end stages can be very difficult. You may experience a wide range of emotions including, but not limited to, disbelief, fear, sadness, anger, relief, etc. Eventually, however, you will need to accept your diagnosis.

Processing the Initial Diagnosis

When your doctor first gives you a diagnosis, it may be difficult for your mind to process. If it is an unexpected diagnosis, the shock may prevent you from asking important questions, or even giving a response at this initial appointment. You may need to take a few days to digest this new information, but be sure to schedule a follow-up appointment to discuss the diagnosis and prognosis further.

Once you have had some time to come to terms with your new diagnosis, there are some questions you need to ask:

> How did my doctor determine this diagnosis?
> Is my doctor a specialist in this diagnostic area?
> Should I seek a second opinion?

These are all legitimate questions to consider.

It is important that your doctor explains clearly how your diagnosis was reached and reviews the results of any medical testing, lab work, or diagnostic exams with you. Make sure to ask questions if you are unclear about any information presented and request a copy of all lab work, radiology reports, and/or test results.

If your doctor does not specialize in your illness, you need to request a referral to someone who does. A primary care physician (PCP) cannot possibly keep up with all of the new research and developments within the medical field, but someone who specializes in your condition has the expertise and updated knowledge to know all of the newest treatment options.

Do not be afraid to request additional testing and/or a second opinion. You do not have to accept this initial diagnosis blindly or be afraid you may hurt your doctor's feelings by requesting a consultation with a specialist.

Stages of Acceptance

Once you have enough medical information to confirm that your diagnosis is accurate, you may begin to experience many different emotions. Individuals who have received a chronic or terminal diagnosis often transition through several emotional stages as they attempt to process and then accept their illness. Though I have numbered the stages, each person is different and you may not experience them all, or in the order outlined.

Stage 1:   Denial and Disbelief

Stage 2:   Anger

Stage 3:   Bargaining

Stage 4:   Depression

Stage 5:   Acceptance

I believe it is important to be familiar with these stages in order to better understand and accept the emotions you may be feeling. What follows is a brief overview along with personal examples to illustrate each stage.

Denial and Disbelief

In the initial stage, Denial and Disbelief, your mind may reject the reality of your new diagnosis. This is a natural reaction, especially if you are not experiencing any symptoms, or if your symptoms are mild. You may not even realize you are in denial, but as your mind has time to process this new information, it should eventually accept your diagnosis.

I experienced my second collapsed lung in March of 2006. My convalescence lasted until early May, and by the time I returned to work on a part-time basis, the semester was almost over. Working at a university, I had the summer months off, so I didn't return to full-time employment until the following August.

Over that summer, my pulmonary function tests (PFTs) plummeted, my chest discomfort worsened, and I was diagnosed with diabetes. My body was screaming that I needed to slow down, but I chose not to acknowledge it. I started to postpone or cancel appointments with my doctors because I could not handle the medical decline that was documented there.

By early December, I was really struggling, and after several weeks of oral antibiotics, my doctor recommended hospitalization. Reality came crashing down on me. My doctor explained that my lung functions had dropped low enough to qualify me for a lung transplant and said I needed to seriously consider going on disability. I had to finally acknowledge my failing health and make some difficult decisions.

Anger

Many people will transition from denial to anger. It is hard not to feel angry when you have received a difficult medical diagnosis. You may believe it isn't fair, or ask, "Why me?"

This anger can often be channeled toward others. I am sure you have heard the expression, "misery loves company," and in a situation like this, you may feel like everyone should be as miserable as you are. It is important to try to work through this stage as quickly as possible, for your sake and the sake of those around you.

During my January hospitalization I truly mourned my loss. I was hurt and angry that I had to give up the job I loved so much. I questioned why something like this was happening to me; what had I done to deserve this?

Normally I have a very even temperament, but I became very irritable during this time. It seemed like nothing my husband or daughter did was good enough. My feelings of anger and disappointment seemed to consume me.

It took my daughter's tears and questions about why I kept yelling at her to make me realize I was taking my irritation out on her. It forced me to change my mental attitude.

Bargaining

Bargaining is a stage often experienced by those of faith. Someone who is in the bargaining stage may pray, "God, if you heal me, I will be a better friend, parent, spouse, or person." There is nothing wrong with praying for healing, but you need to realize, your illness is not a punishment God has given you for something you have or have not done.

There have been many times during the years when I have entered this bargaining stage, often when my health was declining. I would pray:

- ✧ "Please God, if you make my PFTs go up, I will do more respiratory treatments each day."
- ✧ "Lord, if you would just let me get better, I will cut back on my responsibilities at work."
- ✧ "Jesus, if you give me the strength to attend this event, I will never ask for anything again."

I have gradually learned that bargaining is not going to change my condition or make me healthier. My prayers are better served by asking for the ability to cope with and accept my failing health.

Depression

As we move closer to the final stage, Acceptance, we may begin to experience a sense of sadness, fear, or anxiety about what is to come. These feelings of depression are normal and okay. Your mind is trying to cope with a new negative reality, and this can be extremely difficult.

As I have progressed through my illness, I have moved in and out of depression many times, often simultaneously with other stages. With each medical setback, I have experienced fear and sadness.

The summer after my lung collapsed, I started having horrible anxiety attacks. Anytime I felt discomfort or pain in my chest, my mind over-reacted and jumped to the conclusion that my lung had collapsed again. I finally explained what was happening to my doctor, and he was able to prescribe an anti-depressant to help control the anxiety I was feeling.

Following my early retirement from St. Bonaventure, I became extremely depressed. While my family was gone to school and work, I moped around the house crying and sleeping. I was feeling sorry for myself and dwelling on all of the things I could no longer do. With the help of my family, some good friends, and a lot of prayer, I finally pulled myself out of this stage and progressed to the final stage, Acceptance.

Learning how to cope with your anxiety and depression is very important and will be addressed in a later chapter. If your depression or anxiety begins to interfere with your ability to function, you need to seek professional assistance. Your doctor can help by referring you to a counselor or psychologist in your community.

Acceptance

The final stage is Acceptance, coming to terms with your condition; accepting it for what it is; and choosing to make the most of it. This is the stage we all want to achieve, but it is not an easy road to get there.

Once I finally entered the stage of acceptance, I could return to living my life and appreciating the things I could still do. With a positive mental attitude, I was able to cope with my physical symptoms better and find ways to enjoy the modified life I was living. I was also able to help those around me begin to accept my decline and find acceptance themselves.

We are each unique individuals, so your experiences may differ from mine. I would encourage you to start a journal to record the feelings and experiences you are having. Through this journal, you can identify your own emotions and better understand where you are on the journey toward acceptance.

The strategies outlined in the following chapters can serve as a road map to guide you toward acceptance of your chronic or terminal condition.

CHAPTER TWO

Taking Control

One of the keys to successfully coping with a chronic illness is to take control of your health. This should become your top priority. You need to become the foremost expert on your condition, but where do you begin?

Educate Yourself

Once you have a diagnosis, you should learn as much about your illness as possible. Start by asking your doctors questions. Pick up informational brochures while you are in their offices and ask if they have any recommendations for good books you could read to help you become better educated.

The Internet is a great tool; however, use it cautiously. When you are reading a medical journal, you know the information has been researched and submitted to a stringent review process. General articles on-line cannot boast this same level of screening, so be careful what you choose to believe.

Many chronic illnesses have foundations to support research and advances. Search out the official websites for your condition and use them as a resource for finding other reputable sites. (A list of several helpful sites can be found in the Resources Section at the end of the book).

On-line chat rooms and community boards are often intriguing, but, again, these are individuals giving their own opinions and experiences. Though it is often comforting to read about other people who are experiencing what you are, do not depend on them for expert advice.

Prepare a Detailed Medical History

It is helpful if you can type or write a detailed medical history. Your medical history should include your name, medical condition(s), and date of birth; an updated list of medications; all physician information; a history of previous hospitalizations; and any important additional medical information. See sample:

Medical History:				Diabetic Health Supply		
Mary May Advocate	COPD and Diabetes	**12/01/1967**		90 Carbonot Dr. Sugarville, NY 12123	Phone: (323) 889-9900	
Medication:		**Dose/Frequency:**				
Pulmozyme 2.5mg		1 x per day		**Hospital Name:**	**Dates:**	**Reason:**
Xopenex HFA 45 mcg		2 puffs 2x per day		Happyville General Hospital	5/23 to 5/26 2008	Flu
Advair 500/50		1 puff 2x per day		400 Good Health Ave.		
Humalog		1 unit per 15 carbs		Happyville, NY 16980		
Lantus		18 units at night		HGH	5/3 to 5/6 2008	Pneumonia
Azithromycin 500 mg		3x per week		HGH	4/7 to 4/12 2008	Pneumonia
Prevacid 30		1x per day		Women's Hospital of Sugarville	1/19 to 1/26 2008	Pneumonia
Prozac		1x per day		300 Main St.		
				Sugarville, NY 12123		
Physicians:				WHS	1/3 to 1/14 2008	Sinus Surgery
Dr. Good Lungfellow				HGH	9/20 to 9/27 2007	Gastroenteritis
Happyville Medical Group						
535 Main St.		Phone: (101) 222-3333		University Medical Center	3/15 to 3/28 2006	Pneumothorax
Happyville, NY 16980		Fax: (101) 223-3232		219 Helping Way		VATS Pleurodesis
				Mercyville, PA 13232		
Dr. Max Glucosamine				UMC	2/23 to 3/2 2005	IV antibiotics
Endocrinology Associates		Phone: (212) 648-6311				
130 Sugarland Drive		Fax: (212) 648-6369		HGH	4/3 to 4/15 2002	Pneumothorax
Maplehurst, NY 18029						
Other Health Care Providers:						
Happyville Home Health Services						
335 Good Health Ave.		Phone: (101) 345-6677				
Happyville, NY 16980						

Keep a copy of this medical history with you at all times so it will be easy to access if you need emergency care.

Begin a Medical Journal

Use a journal to record any changes in symptoms, questions that come up between doctor visits, and important contact information (physicians, pharmacy numbers, home health providers, etc.). I would also recommend you keep within this journal a copy of your medical history and any advance directives (a living will, health care proxy, power of attorney, or DNR; these will be discussed in greater detail in Chapter Five).

Create a Personal Medical File

Keeping all of your medical information organized and in one place will help you manage your care. Your personal medical file should include discharge summaries from hospitalizations, copies of lab reports and other medical testing (be sure to request a copy of the results at the time of the procedure), correspondence from your physicians, prescriptions you need to fill, information about the drugs you are taking and their side-effects, and any other pertinent medical information.

You should keep a separate section in your medical file to save receipts and bills you have paid.

Make sure to keep the original pharmacy receipts; note the date and type of payment used on any paid medical bills.

Many employers offer flexible spending programs for their employees. With a flexible spending account, money is deducted from your salary at the beginning of the year, before taxes, and you submit medical receipts for reimbursement.

If you do not have the option of a flexible spending account, the Federal Government also offers tax deductions for medical spending over a certain amount yearly, based on your annual income. Keep a detailed record of, and all receipts from, any medical spending.

Become an Active Member of Your Medical Team

As an individual with chronic illness, it is extremely important for you to become an active participant in the medical process. Too often patients take a passive role in their health care, leaving all decision-making to the medical staff. You cannot afford to do this. You and the medical professionals should work together to improve your health; this is a team approach, and you need to be an equal partner.

A positive relationship with your doctor is essential. If you do not feel comfortable speaking with your doctor, asking questions, and giving your input, you need to consider finding a new doctor. The doctors are working for you. You have the final say in all health care management, so make sure your doctor respects your desires and encourages your involvement in treatment plans.

One way to keep an active relationship with doctors between appointments is to ask if they would be willing to provide you with their e-mail address. E-mail can be a wonderful tool for communicating with your medical team, when used responsibly. Obviously, in an emergency situation, contacting your doctor by phone is the only option, but for general medical questions or to periodically check in, e-mail is a good alternative; it gives doctors the freedom to respond when they are able.

Many doctors' offices have a nurse coordinator. Often this person serves as the go between for patients and doctors and is a wonderful resource (friend, savior, support person, listener...) for you. Make sure to ask if your doctor has a nurse coordinator and add this person's contact information to your medical journal.

If at all possible, it is always a good idea to bring a support person with you to doctor appointments. This serves several purposes. First, doctor visits can be stressful and cause anxiety; bringing a support person along for encouragement can help reduce these feelings. Second, it is always good to have another set of ears. It can be hard to process all the new information presented, especially if it is negative. Having an extra person there to listen and ask questions can be extremely helpful. Finally, your support person can take notes for you during the appointment to be reviewed later.

Don't forget to bring your medical journal with you to all appointments so you can report any new symptoms; refer to the questions you have recorded; and write down any new contact information, prescriptions, or follow-up appointments you need to make. If your doctor is ordering new lab work or testing, remember to request a copy of the results for your personal medical file.

Understand Your Insurance Coverage

Becoming knowledgeable about your insurance coverage is critical. Many plans differ in the amount of coverage, cost of co-pays, need for prior-authorization for treatment, and use of referrals. Some important questions to ask your insurance provider:

➢ Do I need to designate a primary care physician (PCP)?

➢ Does my PCP have to refer me to specialists?

➢ Do I need prior authorization for things like home health, hospitalization, and other medical treatments and procedures? If yes, am I responsible for requesting this, or is my doctor?

➢ What will my out-of-pocket expenses be for doctor's office visits, specialist visits, prescriptions, hospitalization, emergency care, etc.?

➤ What items are not covered by my insurance (eye exams, mental health counseling, durable medical equipment, home health nursing, inpatient rehabilitation, Hospice, etc.)?

➤ Is there a Lifetime Maximum Benefit? (This is a very important question to ask. Many insurance companies set a lifetime cap and if your medical spending surpasses it, you lose your benefits.)

Make sure you keep all correspondence with your insurance company, including records of what they have paid and what you are responsible for; notices of authorization of services; and written notes about any verbal conversations you have had with their representatives including the date, name of the agent, and what was discussed.

Localize Your Prescriptions

We have all heard horror stories of people having severe, or even fatal reactions, to a combination of incompatible prescription drugs. This can occur when you have multiple physicians prescribing for you. By choosing one pharmacy to handle all of your medication needs, you can avoid dangerous drug interactions.

Your pharmacy maintains a record of all the drugs you are taking and any incompatibilities between your prescribed medications, allowing your pharmacist to alert you and your doctor about any dangerous drug combinations. Your pharmacist can also help you decide what over-the-counter medications will work best for you based on your medical condition and medication list.

Do not depend on your physicians to catch incompatible medications, especially if you have several doctors treating different conditions. Make sure you bring your updated medical history with you to all doctors' appointments, so the medications in your file can be reviewed and updated.

Establish a good relationship with your pharmacist and don't be afraid to ask questions and discuss any concerns you have about your medications.

Invest in a Medical Alert ID

Anyone with a chronic condition including, but not limited to: asthma, diabetes, epilepsy, heart disease, hypertension, and/or allergies should own a Medical Alert ID. This will immediately notify medical personnel of your condition(s). There are many ID options available.

Commit and be Compliant

You will not maintain any level of health if you do not commit to your own medical care. I realize that chronic illness often brings with it new responsibilities, medications, and treatment plans, but you must learn to accept these additions to your daily routine and stick to them.

We all have slip-ups, and you will not be perfect, but doing your best to stay compliant will help you avoid more serious complications.

When people are feeling sick, they tend to be better at compliance than when they are feeling healthy. The problem is, if you do not continue to follow your medical plan, even when you are feeling good, your condition will only worsen.

Here are some tips to help you remember to follow your treatment plan:

Prepare a Weekly Schedule

If you are having difficulty remembering to take medications or to do necessary treatments, set up a schedule for yourself and place it in a prominent location.

Set an Alarm

Many cell phones and watches offer alarm systems that can be set to remind you when your treatments are due.

Pair Your Medications With Other Routine Activities

Try pairing your medications or treatments with other daily activities like meals, work breaks, or bedtime.

Keep Your Prescriptions Organized and in an Accessible Location

Pill minders are a wonderful way to keep track of your medications. Having multiple pill bottles to deal with daily may lead to confusion, so carefully filling a pill minder once a week will help you avoid forgetting something.

It is also important to make sure your medications are in a location that will be accessible at the times you need to take them. For example, if the drug you are taking is prescribed for before bed, keep it in your bedroom, not downstairs in the kitchen. (Who wants to hike back downstairs when you are settled snuggly in bed?)

You are the key to good management of your illness. It doesn't matter how good your health care is, if you are not willing to commit fully to your own care, your quality of life will severely suffer.

CHAPTER THREE

Sharing with Family & Friends

A few years ago my father-in-law was diagnosed with Stage IV Melanoma. In October of 2003, following surgeries and treatments that seemed to put the cancer into remission, a malignant brain tumor was discovered. Despite many radiation treatments, Dad succumbed to the cancer and died February 2, 2004.

Dad was a successful business owner, well liked by the community, and had many close friends. When he initially received the diagnosis of brain cancer, he entered the first stage, Denial and Disbelief.

Dad was unable to work; yet, he never shared with his employees what he was dealing with. His friends were also kept in the dark about the severity of his condition. Those of us in his immediate family were not allowed to share his prognosis with others or our concerns about his failing health.

As we watched Dad's illness progress, we tried to discuss with him issues about the business and finances, but he refused to talk about these things. By the time Dad finally realized and accepted he was dying (one week before his death), it was too late to discuss his final wishes because he was too sick to communicate them to us.

When Dad passed away, his friends, employees, and extended family were totally shocked. Most of them knew Dad was sick, but none of them realized he was terminal. They were devastated by his death. Friends and family didn't have the opportunity to share with Dad how much he had meant to them, be there during those last few months, offer support, or say goodbye.

I know Dad chose not to share because he didn't want to burden other people, but by keeping his struggles to himself, he lost valuable opportunities with his family and friends. I can still sense his friends' regret anytime they speak of my dear father-in-law.

Honest Communication is Critical

There are several reasons why individuals recently diagnosed with chronic or terminal illness do not share with their family or friends. For some, saying it out loud makes it real and they would prefer to remain in denial. Others are afraid they will burden or upset their families by sharing their diagnosis. Fear of being pitied or fussed over can be another deterrent.

None of us want to be a burden or to upset our family, but our family is often our main base of support. They need and deserve to know the truth about your diagnosis and prognosis. If you are not personally comfortable sharing this with family members, bring them to your next doctor's appointment and let your doctor educate them. Any pamphlets or reading materials you were given about your condition should also be shared with the members of your family.

Preparing for Their Reaction

Family members may experience similar emotional stages to your own and will need their own support system. Denying them the ability to share with their friends or other close family members will only make the acceptance process more difficult.

Your friends will also want to be able to support you as you deal with your illness. They may feel hurt and surprised if they find out from someone other than you, so take the time to speak with each of them individually.

Do not be surprised if your family members or friends' reaction is to deny the seriousness of your condition, especially if your diagnosis is terminal. It is very difficult for our loved ones to accept the reality that we are dying. You may have to assist them with this, once you have found personal acceptance of your diagnosis.

I had to have a serious conversation with both of my parents that included my telling them, in no uncertain terms, that I was dying. (Don't be surprised if they tell you, "Don't say that!"). This is extremely hard, but your family needs to accept what is happening in order to cope and assist you with your illness process.

There are many community resources available to assist your family including counselors, support groups, and Hospice services.

Plan for the Future

Regardless of whether or not your condition is terminal, making a plan for the future and discussing it with your family is a smart thing to do.

Prepare a Will

If you have never drawn up a will, take the time to do so, especially if you have children. If you do not have a will, you are leaving decisions about the affairs of your estate to the government.

Discuss Finances

Address with your family members any insurance policies you may hold, bank account information, and debt you owe. Keep the paperwork to these accounts in a safe place, but make sure your family knows where to find them. Also make sure they have been given authorization to access them if you are unable.

Complete Advance Directives

Make sure you have completed some kind of advance directive. Types of advance directives include a living will, power of attorney, health care proxy, or DNR (do not resuscitate order). These types of directives will assist your family in making difficult medical decisions if you are not able and will be discussed in more detail in Chapter Five.

Record End of Life Wishes

All of us are going to die, so leaving instructions for your family about burial choices, memorial and funeral desires, or any last requests is a wonderful gift you can give them during their time of mourning.

Involving your family and friends in your coping process will not only help you, but will bring them peace and comfort. Do not wait until it is too late to discuss these important matters with them.

CHAPTER FOUR

Talking to Your Children

This topic is, by far, the most sensitive and difficult one to deal with. As a parent, I have struggled with knowing how to discuss my terminal illness with my daughter, Hannah. Certainly the age and maturity of your children makes a huge difference in how you go about explaining your condition to them.

Some questions you may want to answer prior to deciding how to approach this topic with your children include:

What is the extent of your symptoms? Are you visibly ill, or is your illness currently hidden?

Depending on the stage your illness is in, you may or may not have symptoms. Prior to developing symptoms, it may be difficult to explain to younger children that Mommy or Daddy is sick, but once you begin to have visible symptoms, communication with your children is crucial. Trying to protect your children will only make them unsure and fearful. Educating them about your symptoms will help them cope better with your progressing illness.

Is your prognosis terminal?

If your illness is terminal, you need to prepare your children for what is to come. You do not want to scare them, but need to begin a dialogue about death and dying.

Some helpful tools you can use to approach this topic are children's literature addressing loss and coping, movies illustrating the death of a parent (Disney offers many of these), or spiritual stories explaining about God and Heaven.

Start by discussing death in a generalized way with your children, using the tools I have mentioned. When you encounter loss in a story or movie, stop and ask your children questions about how they would feel, what they would do, and remind them that the child in the story is going to be okay and well cared for.

Be careful what metaphors you use to explain death to a child. Telling a child, "When someone dies they go to sleep and never wake up," may cause the child to fear sleep and bedtime.

As a person of faith, I have been able to discuss with my daughter God's love for us, the joy and beauty of Heaven, and the promise we will be together there some day.

It is important to be as positive as possible. Remind your children that you want them to be happy and to go on with their lives. Tell them how much you love them and that your love will always be with them. Surround them with people who care about and love them to offer support and comfort.

I believe a wonderful gift you can leave for your children is either a video or written journal. Share with them the life lessons you have learned. Tell them about your childhood experiences. Warn them about pitfalls you may have encountered so they can be wary of having those same bad experiences. Document the time you have had with them and the memories of things you have done together.

If you have not yet entered the stage of acceptance, many of these suggestions may be extremely difficult for you. If this is the case, make sure there are other people helping you to prepare your children.

How many people know about your condition?

Decisions on what and how much to tell your children may depend on how public your condition is.

My illness became widely publicized when my friends started holding community fundraisers to help with our growing medical expenses. Several articles were written about me in the local papers and, suddenly, most of the families in our community knew about, and were discussing with their children, my condition. Had I not shared with my daughter, Hannah, what was happening, she may have heard about it from someone else and been scared and confused.

Because I had been honest with Hannah, she was able to come to me to discuss things other children said to her; like the day one of her friends told her, "My mommy said your mommy is going to die tonight." Although this was very upsetting for her, at least she wasn't afraid to come to me and talk about it. I was able to help Hannah laugh about the situation by waking her up the following morning with the words, "Guess what? You can tell Sammy that your mommy survived the night!"

How can I help my children cope?

One of the worst things you can do is not say anything to your children. Kids are very perceptive and if they sense something is wrong, which they will, they may believe they are at fault in some way.

There are many ways you can begin to help your children cope with your illness. Some possibilities are:

Take Them With You to a Doctor's Appointment
(Make sure you have warned your doctor in advance.)

Two years ago I had a spontaneous pneumothorax (collapsed lung) and had to be hospitalized for two weeks. When I came home, Hannah experienced a great deal of separation anxiety. She cried every day getting on the bus to go to school and wouldn't leave my side when she was at home. It was obvious she was terrified something bad was going to happen again.

Once I knew my condition was stable and things were going well, I asked my doctor if I could bring Hannah with me to my next appointment. My health care team was willing and did a wonderful job explaining to her what had happened and reassured her that I was okay. When we left my doctor's office she seemed happy and relieved.

After the appointment we visited a *Build A Bear Workshop* and picked out a bunny that we named Cheer Me Up. Hannah and I worked on her together, and I gave Cheer Me Up's heart a special kiss with my love in it so, even when I couldn't be there, Hannah would have my love with her. She took Cheer Me Up to

school with her the rest of that year and half of the next;
her tears and anxiety never returned.

Teach Them About Your Condition

There are many excellent children's books that
explain different chronic conditions.   Your doctor's
office may have some literature, but if they don't, look at
your local library, bookstore, or search on-line. Helping
your child to understand your illness will make it less
foreign and terrifying.

Get Them Involved in Your Care

This can be as simple as having them help you fill
your pill minder each week. Any kind of control you
can give your children will help them accept your
medical condition.

When I was diagnosed with diabetes, I showed
Hannah my blood sugar monitor and we checked her
blood so she could experience what it felt like to get her

finger pricked. She thought that was great and wanted to check her sugar each time I did.

Give Them More Responsibility Around the House

As your condition deteriorates, you may need more assistance with household tasks. By starting your children's involvement in household chores early, before your symptoms become more severe, they will become more self-sufficient, able to function without your constant care, and won't blame their increased responsibilities on you or your illness.

Involve Them in a Support Group for Children of Parents with Chronic Illness

Having a group of friends to talk to who understand what they are going through can be very beneficial for your children. Many schools offer these types of support groups; contact the guidance counselor to inquire about school-sponsored programs.

Seek Professional Assistance

If your children are struggling, get them an appointment to see a child psychologist or family counselor. The counselor and/or psychologist at the school can also serve as wonderful support people for your children and an excellent resource for you.

You know your children best. Be creative in the ways you help them cope and tailor strategies to their individual ages and needs.

CHAPTER FIVE

Hospitalization

Hospitalization is, unfortunately, a common experience for many individuals with chronic illness. Though this isn't something most of us enjoy, it is a necessary part of our care. There are many ways you can make hospitalizations less stressful.

Preparing for Hospitalization

Prior to hospitalization, it is important to keep your medical history updated. Each time you add or subtract a medication, physician, or other medical service be sure to change it in your history. Bring your medical journal, including a copy of your medical history, with you to the hospital for reference while answering admission questions.

It is a good idea to find one or two support people who would be able to be with you during your hospital stay. It is important to educate them about your medications and condition so they will be able to advocate for you if you are unable.

Advance Directives

It is imperative for you to complete advance directives before hospitalization. Each state has preferences for the type of advance directives their hospitals use, so be sure to consult with the hospital about what is recommended. There are several forms of advance directives including a power of attorney, living will, health care proxy, or do not resuscitate orders (DNR). These documents let your physicians know who is responsible for making decisions for you if you are unable. Advance directive forms can be obtained from the hospital social worker or patient advocate.

Power of Attorney

You use a power of attorney to appoint an agent to make health care decisions for you if you are unable, regardless of the terminality of your condition. Your agent may need to authorize admission to, or discharge from, the hospital and/or consent for treatments such as surgery.

Living Will

A living will outlines your decisions regarding life-sustaining measures and only takes effect if your medical condition becomes terminal with no sign of recovery.

Health Care Proxy

A health care proxy is someone you have appointed to make sure your end of life medical wishes are upheld. Unlike the power of attorney, a health care proxy is only responsible for end of life decisions. Make sure your appointed agent is aware of your wishes for life support, organ donation, and other important medical issues.

Do Not Resuscitate Order

Finally, a DNR is a written document placed in your medical chart instructing hospital personnel to hold off on CPR and other life-sustaining measures if your heart or breathing stops.

Being a Good Self-Advocate

Once you have been admitted to the hospital, your job as an active team member does not stop. During your hospital stay you must advocate for your own needs, but in an appropriate way. Avoid becoming a *Too Nice Nancy* or a *Grouchy Gretchen.*

You may know a person like *Too Nice Nancy* (I know her all too well, she used to be me!) who is more concerned about everyone liking her than about receiving good medical care. Nancy never rings her call bell, would rather lie awake at night listening to her IV beep than disturb her nurse, doesn't report her discomfort unless specifically asked, and ends up having an EKG when she needed a chest X-Ray because she was too afraid to speak up. When she is finally discharged, the nurses rave about how easy she was, while she cries in the car on the way home due to the discomfort of bedsores on her bottom.

Grouchy Gretchen, on the other hand, is a nurse's worst nightmare. She is grumpy and demanding from the moment she gets on the floor. Gretchen believes if she is miserable, everyone else should be too, so she complains to anyone who will listen. She yells at her respiratory therapist about her breakfast; rings her call bell at her whim to demand food, drinks, and attention; complains to her doctor about how poorly she is being treated and how inept her nurses are; and refuses to take medications and treatments because she doesn't like them. Toward the end of her stay, nurses are drawing straws to see who gets stuck caring for her, and everyone on the floor (including staff and patients) rejoices when she is wheeled out the door.

To be a good self-advocate, you must find a middle ground between Nancy and Gretchen. Here are some helpful tips:

Only Use Your Call Light When You Really Need Assistance

It is okay to ring the call bell, but only do so when you really need the nurse's assistance. For example, use the call bell if your IV is alarming, you start to feel worse or have unusual symptoms, you need help getting to the bathroom, or you need medication.

If you believe you are in need of emergent assistance, make this very clear when you communicate with the nurse's station. Unless you need immediate help, if you ring the call bell and no one comes after 15 to 20 minutes, press it again. You are not the only patient on the floor and the nurse will get to you as soon as she can, but nurses also get caught up in other situations and may forget you called, so don't be afraid to ring out after a reasonable time has passed.

Pay Attention to the Treatments and Medications You are Receiving

If anything is missing from your normal routine, tell your nurse about it. Sometimes orders get mistyped or medications get accidentally skipped over. If this happens, review the list of medications with your nurse to be sure it is accurate. Also, pay attention to dosing; too few or too many pills can be a serious problem, SPEAK UP!

Often new medications may be tried while you are in the hospital. If these medications are not familiar to you, ask the doctor for information about them. If any medications are brought for you that were not discussed by your doctor, ask why you are being given them BEFORE you take them. If the nurse is unsure, have her contact your doctor for confirmation prior to administration.

If You are Experiencing Pain, Give an Honest Assessment Based on the Hospital Pain Scale

People with chronic illness often have greater pain tolerance, but don't underestimate the level of your pain just to be brave or seem tough. There is nothing wrong with asking for pain medication; it will help you cope better and allow you to rest.

Keep a List of Questions or Problems to Address with Your Doctors Each Day

Typically, your doctor will only visit you once a day while you are in the hospital, so it is important to make the most of this time. Keep a list of questions or concerns you would like to address so you won't forget during your doctor's visit.

If the quality of your care is poor, you need to let your doctors know so they can make sure you get the attention you deserve.

Hospital Survival Tips

There are several things you can do to make your hospital stay better; here are some tips I would like to offer you:

Get Plenty of Rest

This may be one of the most difficult things to accomplish during your hospitalization. Nurses and other staff are in and out of your room at all hours of the day and night. It is terribly important, however, that you get enough sleep. The key to this is napping frequently throughout the day. You are in the hospital because you are sick, so there is no reason you can't rest during both the day and night.

Try to limit the number of visitors and phone calls you are receiving. It is wonderful that your friends and family want to support you during your hospitalization, but you are there to get well, not to entertain. Don't be afraid to unplug the phone and/or post a "Do Not Disturb" sign on the door when you are resting.

If you start becoming over-tired, speak with your doctor about possibly changing the nighttime schedule of medications, blood draws, and vital sign checks to allow you a greater stretch of quiet time. If this is not possible, you may want to request something to help your body relax and go to sleep.

Getting run-down in the hospital often leads to further complications or additional infections, so take your rest time very seriously.

Keep Your Body Nourished and Hydrated

I know hospital food is not always the most appealing, but it is very important that you eat and drink plenty daily. You need to maintain your nourishment in order to get stronger. Many hospitals offer alternate menus you can order from if you do not like the main fare. Most floors also stock drinks, snacks, and other food items; don't be afraid to ask your nursing assistant what is available.

If nausea is interfering with your ability to eat, speak with your doctor about medication options that may ease this. If you are not able to ingest enough liquid, ask about the possibility of intravenous fluids.

Get Up and Get Out

If your doctor has cleared you to do so, make it a point to get out of your room and walk. Lying around will make you feel weak and decrease your muscle tone. Even if you only go for short walks a few times a day, it will help your body get stronger.

If you are not able to get out of bed, your risk for developing deep venous thrombosis (blood clots) greatly increases. Discuss preventative therapy options with your doctor to avoid this serious complication.

Bring Your Own Medications

If you take several prescription medications, bring a one-week supply with you to the hospital. Keep it in your bag incase, for some reason, your medication does not come on time or is unavailable. Normally, nurses are happy to re-stock your personal supply once the pharmacy sends the medication to them.

Wash Your Hands

Even if you never leave your room, you can be exposed to germs. Make sure you wash your hands frequently, especially after you use the restroom and before you eat.

Many hospital rooms are equipped with hand sanitizer dispensers, but the alcohol in these dispensers doesn't eliminate soiling from dirt, blood, feces, or other body fluids; these must be washed away with soap and water. Insist that hospital staff, doctors, and visitors wash their hands each time they come into your room.

Hospitals are an easy place to pick up germs and infections like MRSA, VRE, and C. Difficile (resistant organisms that are highly contagious and require isolation and contact precautions); you can never be too cautious.

Keep Yourself Occupied

A hospital stay can be very boring. Be sure to bring things you enjoy to fill the time. Many hospitals have wireless Internet, so a laptop can keep you connected to the rest of the world, allow you to watch DVDs, or do some on-line shopping. (My favorite hospital pastime!)

Most hospital rooms are equipped with free cable televisions, but be careful! Sometimes the wording in the patient handbook can be unclear and may seem to indicate a charge to activate both the phone and television. The television is usually a free service for patients; whereas, the charge per-day for activating your in-room phone can be excessive. Cell phones are permitted in most patient rooms; using a cell phone, if you have one, may be more economical for making outside calls. Your room phone does not need to be activated in order to receive calls, so your friends and family can still contact you.

If you enjoy reading, bring plenty of books and magazines. Music can be a nice distraction as well; consider bringing an MP3 or portable CD player. The entertainment options are unlimited; be creative.

Be Comfortable

Let's face it, hospital gowns are not very comfortable or attractive. Depending on the reason for your hospitalization, you may be able to wear your own clothes instead of a gown. Make sure to pack comfortable clothing like PJ bottoms, warm socks, and fresh underwear (enough for daily changes).

Shoes or slippers that are easy to slide on and off are also good to have at your bedside. Hospital floors can be dirty and sticky; you don't want to walk around with bare feet.

If you tend to get cold, you should pack a robe, fleece, or zip-up sweatshirt that you can cover up with. I also like to bring my own pillow. (The hospital ones can be the pits!)

None of us like to spend time in the hospital, but if you manage this experience well, you can leave feeling better and more in control of your medical condition.

CHAPTER SIX

Managing Your Medical Expenses

Chronic illness can be very expensive. Between the cost of medications, doctor's appointments, hospitalizations, and specialized services, the bills can become overwhelming. Though I am not a money management expert, I would like to share some of the lessons, tips, and resources I have discovered to help manage my medical expenses.

Avoid Using Your Credit Card

Credit cards often seem like an easy fix when you don't have money to cover your expenses, but be careful how frequently you use them to pay your medical costs. If you aren't cautious, you can quickly wrack up a great deal of credit card debt. The interest alone can make paying your accumulated debt seem impossible and, in extreme cases, may lead to bankruptcy.

When I got married, I was a full-time college student and wasn't earning any money. My husband and I were living on a single fixed income, and things were tight. Though we had a health insurance plan through my husband's employer, we had to pay the bills upfront for medical expenses. After, we submitted the receipts and were reimbursed for 80%. The trap we fell into was, when the reimbursement check came, we often used the money to cover other expenses instead of paying off our credit card debt.

When your medications are costing thousands of dollars each month and you have to pay for them out of pocket, it is difficult not to get in the habit of using a credit card. By the time I finished college and started earning a salary, we had already accumulated over $20,000 in credit card debt. It took a great deal of discipline and sacrifice to finally pay off what we owed.

Create a Budget and Stick to It

All of us have monthly expenses, but those with chronic illness have the additional cost of medical care. If you have fixed monthly medical expenses, you need to factor these costs into your family's budget, but you also need to keep in mind, there could be unexpected medical costs during the month as well.

Creating a separate account to cover your medical expenses can be helpful. In this account you can keep the money to cover your monthly medical bills and deposit any extra money left over each month from your family account. Think of it as a savings account to be used for any unforeseen medical expenses.

People save money for many different reasons: retirement, children's college tuition, vacations, etc. As a person with chronic illness, you should be saving money for medical emergencies so you don't end up with significant debt.

Don't Be Afraid to Accept Help from Others

As my medical expenses have grown, my friends have reached out to help me by holding fundraisers. At first, I felt guilty asking people in the community for money. We live a middle class life style, have a nice home, and a comfortable standard of living, but with my early retirement, a large monthly mortgage payment, and rising medical costs, we were financially overwhelmed.

My friends organized a walk, a benefit, and several other smaller fundraisers to help with my medical expenses. The outpouring of community support both amazed and deeply touched me. People want to help others in need and are often very generous when they feel their money is going to a worthy cause. The money donated has taken a huge strain off our family and has allowed me to put aside money to cover my upcoming transplant costs.

Research Disability Insurance Options

If you are currently working full-time, but fear you may have to retire early because of your medical condition, you may want to inquire as to whether your employer has a Long Term Disability (LTD) Program and/or Disability Insurance.

An LTD policy typically pays you a percentage of your monthly salary while you are permanently disabled; this income is taxed.

Disability Insurance is a supplemental plan that pays a fixed amount monthly, over and above any other benefits you are receiving, and is not taxed.

I was fortunate enough to work for an employer who offered both options. I was able, despite my pre-existing condition, to enroll in the Disability Insurance Plan at an equitable rate during an open enrollment period. The combination of these two plans has allowed me to continue to receive approximately 85% of my monthly pre-disability salary.

Government Assistance Programs

There are many programs offered by the Federal Government to assist individuals with chronic illness. What follows is a brief overview. For more in-depth information, visit the Social Security website at www.socialsecurity.gov or contact your local Social Security office.

Supplemental Security Income (SSI)

SSI is a program that pays monthly benefits to adults, children, and the elderly with disabilities who have limited income and resources. No work history is needed to apply for this benefit.

Social Security Disability Insurance (SSDI)

SSDI is a disability benefits program for individuals, and their families, who have worked long enough in positions that paid Social Security taxes. Your eligibility for this program is based on the number of work credits you have earned. Work credits are calculated using your annual income and the number of years you worked. Each year the government sends out Social Security Statements that alert you to how many work credits you have received.

In order to receive either SSI or SSDI benefits, you must apply and qualify as an individual with a disability. According to the Social Security Administration, an individual is considered disabled if s/he is unable to work. Your eligibility for disability will be determined by the following rules: "You cannot do work that you did before; you cannot adjust to other work because of your medical condition; and your disability has lasted or is expected to last for at least one year or result in death" (Social Security's Disability Planner, available online at www.socialsecurity.gov).

Family Benefits

If you qualify for Social Security benefits, your spouse and/or children may also be eligible. Contact your local Social Security office for details.

Medicaid

Medicaid is a health insurance plan funded by both the State and Federal government to provide insurance for low-income and disabled individuals and their families. Medicaid is available to working people with disabilities if their "net income is less than 250 percent of the national poverty level" based on family size (www.socialsecurity.gov/disabilityresearch/wi/buyin.htm).

Medicare

Medicare is an insurance program for those who are receiving Social Security retirement benefits or disability benefits. Individuals who have been approved for SSDI will automatically qualify for Medicare two years from the date they began receiving disability payments.

You can apply for Social Security Disability benefits on-line, by telephone, or at your local Social Security Office. I would recommend that you prepare in advance by gathering the appropriate documentation (your personal medical file will come in handy). The list of information you should have can be found on the Social Security website.

When I first began the application process, I was very nervous and confused. I had heard many rumors and myths, which I will share with you.

Myth 1: You have to be disabled for at least a year before you can apply for benefits.

This is false! Apply as soon as you become disabled. The criterion is that your disability must be expected to last at least a year.

Myth 2: You need to hire a lawyer to file for disability benefits.

This is absolutely not the case. As long as you are thorough and have kept good records, you can successfully apply for benefits. However, if your application is denied, you may want to consult with an attorney to assist you with the appeals process.

Myth 3: It will take a year or more for your application to be processed.

If you go into the process well organized and prepared, and your physicians provide their medical information in a timely way, it should take no more than 5 to 6 months. There are many helpful worksheets available at the Social Security website to assist you in gathering the information you will need to begin. The more thorough you can be with your records, the better.

Myth 4: Once you qualify for Disability Benefits, any income you make will disqualify you from receiving your benefits.

You can earn up to $940 per month without jeopardizing your SSDI benefits.

Dealing with a chronic or terminal illness is stressful enough; adding financial strain will only make things harder. The sooner you can begin to plan for how you will cover future medical expenses, the better.

CHAPTER SEVEN

Coping

Learning how to cope with your illness will improve your quality of life and mental health. Good mental health is critical when you are dealing with a progressive chronic illness. This chapter is meant to give you strategies to assist you with the coping process.

Change Your Mental Attitude

Most health care professionals will tell you, your attitude about your illness will make or break you. If you have a negative attitude, you will feel worse than if you maintain a positive outlook. I realize it can be difficult to do this, so let me offer you some ideas that have helped me to keep a positive mental attitude.

Do Not Dwell on What You Cannot Do

When we are facing a chronic condition, it is easy to focus on the limitations it is causing us, which can certainly lead to depression. Instead of dwelling on what you can't do, try to be grateful for what you can do.

Whenever I start to feel down about my limitations, I remind myself that I can still be a good friend, a loving mother, and a supportive spouse; enjoy a good book or movie; and appreciate the world around me by taking drives in the car, sitting on the deck, or going for a ride down the driveway on my scooter. I can also be an inspiration for others through my attitude, behaviors, and writing.

As you start to focus on what you are able to do, your limitations fade away and you begin to feel better.

Acknowledge and Accept Your Limitations

Once you can appreciate the things you are able to do, it is important that you also accept your limitations. Many of us try to push beyond our limits, but this will only cause exhaustion and further health related complications. You need to be realistic in what you are expecting of yourself and acknowledge that you may need assistance in areas where you were self-sufficient before.

I have had to learn to turn over many of my prior responsibilities including working, grocery shopping, cleaning the house, and even driving. Though I do still drive occasionally, I have learned that when I am in pain or am tired, I am not alert enough to drive a car. It was important for me to acknowledge and accept this to protect myself and others.

Count Your Blessings

When we are sick it is very easy to get into a "poor me" mentality. It is okay to feel sad, discouraged, and even frustrated at times. Your lifestyle has been modified and you may not be able to participate in some of the activities you enjoyed when you were healthy. These feelings are normal but must be resolved quickly.

During my last hospitalization, I was feeling pretty depressed, but as I began to look at the patients around me, I realized how lucky I was. Things could be so much worse.

The man in the hospital room next to mine was a quadriplegic. As I lay awake trying to deal with my own pain, I wondered how I would cope with his diagnosis. I was able to get out of my bed, walk to the bathroom, and feed myself; things he could no longer do.

We don't have to look far to find someone whose suffering seems so much greater than ours. This doesn't minimize our own experience, but should serve as a reminder of the many things we are and can be thankful for.

One of the things that helps me through sad times is reflecting on my many blessings. When we are down, we tend to focus on the negatives in our lives, but by switching our focus to those things we have to be grateful for, it can change our whole attitude.

Believe me, I have much more to be thankful for than to complain about. I am loved and prayed for by many people; have a wonderful and supportive family; friends who genuinely care about me; a beautiful home that is bright and cheery, even on the darkest days; a daughter who can make me smile when I'm grumpy; a husband whose hugs and snuggles wrap me up and make me feel special. I could go on and on. The next time you begin to feel low, I would encourage you to start your own list of blessings.

Create New Favorite Activities

It is easy to start feeling left out when your chronic condition worsens. Activities you used to enjoy are no longer accessible to you. Your family and friends' lives continue to be normal, while yours is slowing down. You may become bogged down with self-pity, feeling alone and unneeded, but it is important to work on re-framing this experience. Rather than focusing on the activities you can no longer do, create a new set of activities you CAN do.

I may not be able to ride bikes with Hannah, but I can make crafts with her, play card and board games, color, tell her tricks to perform in the pool or on the trampoline, and participate in her life in a different way than I did before.

I loved going to see bands with my husband, but no longer have the energy for the late night music scene. What I have discovered is, we can still enjoy live music by attending an early happy hour, yet still get me home by my 9:00 bedtime.

I have always enjoyed cinema and theatre, yet often don't have the stamina to get out to a show. We solved that problem by turning our Family Room into a movie theater with a big screen, surround sound, and HD. I can watch all of the new releases in the comfort of my own home.

Entertaining has always been a real pleasure for me, but as my condition has worsened, I haven't been able to prepare meals or even appetizers for our friends and family. It has also become difficult for me to go to other people's homes for the evening; it is too exhausting. The solution I've found is a combination of the two. Our friends and family prepare the food and bring it to our house so we can all enjoy time together.

Be creative and see how many new activities you can add to your life.

Dealing with Anxiety

Anxiety is a common experience for individuals dealing with chronic illness. It can be extremely traumatic and scary if you are not used to feeling anxious. It is important to be able to identify the symptoms of anxiety and learn how to deal with them. Some of the most common symptoms of anxiety include shortness of breath, chest pain or discomfort, restlessness, feelings of dread or fear, difficulty concentrating, excessive sweating, stomach upset, and/or muscle tension.

Anxiety is your body's reaction to a threatening situation, real or imagined. In nature we refer to this as the fight or flight response. Your body is preparing to either defend itself or run like hell.

After I had my second collapsed lung, I started experiencing severe anxiety attacks. Anytime I would feel a pain in my chest, my body would over-react, believing there must be a problem. It took some time, effort, and the assistance of an anti-depressant to get me through this difficult period.

As miserable as anxiety can be, there are many approaches you can take to overcome it. Some helpful strategies are listed below.

Learn to Relax

There are many relaxation techniques you can learn to help you when you become anxious.

- *Controlled Breathing:* Using this technique, you can decrease hyperventilation and shortness of breath. Controlled breathing involves focusing on inhaling through your nose and exhaling through your mouth, taking slow deep breaths. When we are anxious, we tend to feel like we cannot catch our breath. By concentrating on deep breathing, you can help yourself regain control.

- *Visualization:* Close your eyes and picture a place that is relaxing for you. Really focus on this image, putting aside your anxious thoughts.

- *Deep Muscle Relaxation:* Learning how to relax is a wonderful coping tool for stressful situations. Deep muscle relaxation involves the tensing and then relaxing of each of the major muscle groups, starting at your feet and working up to your face. This is a technique that requires practice, a focus on breathing, and the use of mental imagery and/or verbal cues. There are many books and websites available that can teach you how to do this.

- *Exercise:* The endorphins produced through exercise are a natural mood enhancer that can provide anxiety relief. I discovered Yoga, which combined physical exercise with meditation, and found it really helped me to relax and overcome some of my anxiety issues.

- *Distraction:* This is a wonderful technique for situational anxiety (temporary situations that cause anxiety like an uncomfortable medical exam or procedure, a closed MRI, or an IV or Picc line insertion). With distraction, you find something to focus on other than the situation you are currently experiencing. One of my friends suggested I try to recite the alphabet or sing a song backwards. I have found this technique to be very helpful.

Seek Professional Assistance

Meeting with a counselor or psychologist who specializes in anxiety issues may be especially helpful. S/he can assist you in identifying and learning the strategies that work best for you.

Talk to Your Doctor

If none of these techniques work for you, or if your anxiety begins to interfere with your sleep or daily functioning, you need to let your doctor know. There are many medications that can be prescribed to relieve anxiety on a short or long term basis.

Finding Support

Dealing with a chronic or terminal illness can be difficult to do by yourself. Seek out support in your community or on-line.

Many hospitals, clinics, and churches offer support groups for individuals with the same or similar conditions to yours. These groups are helpful for many reasons. They allow you to realize you are not alone in the struggles you are facing and provide an opportunity to share your feelings with people who truly understand. They allow you to gain valuable information about doctors and community resources and give you a sense of friendship and belonging.

Hospice offers support for individuals with terminal illness and their families. Hospice employs a team of professionals that includes physicians, nurses, social workers, counselors, home health aides, clergy, therapists, and volunteers. They also provide medical equipment, supplies, and medications, as well as other services related to the specific terminal illness (http://www.hospicenet.org/html/faq.html).

If you have a condition, like mine, where face-to-face patient contact is discouraged due to cross-infection issues, e-mail and on-line chat rooms can be a wonderful support source. I have several friends with CF whom I stay in touch with through e-mail. It is a wonderful way to share experiences, advice, and simply support one another.

Seeking the help of a counselor is also an excellent support strategy. There is nothing wrong with accepting professional assistance. Coping with a chronic or terminal illness can be stressful and cause a great deal of mental anguish and/or confusion. A counselor can offer the appropriate support strategies to help you.

Certainly family and friends can serve as a good support network to comfort and encourage you. Make sure you reach out to them when you are struggling.

Turning to Your Faith

I have chosen to save this as the final section of the chapter on coping, because my faith, hope, and trust in God is, for me, the most important strategy I have employed to deal with my own progressive chronic illness. I do not believe I could have successfully coped with my terminal condition without my faith in a God who loves me, is beside me, and guides me through the trials of my illness. This faith has brought me peace and comfort. Through prayer, worship, and reflection, I have been able to transform my personal suffering into a way to benefit and help others.

I would encourage you to turn to your own personal faith or belief system to help you overcome your own feelings of fear, sadness, depression, anxiety, discomfort, and/or anger.

A Final Message of Hope:

Have you ever wondered why so many people are drawn to and moved by a Randy Pausch (*The Last Lecture*) or a Morrie Schwartz (*Tuesdays with Morrie*)? It is because these men have lived their terminal illness with dignity and joy. They did not constantly ask, "Why me?" but instead accepted what they were given and made the most of it.

We are all going to die, but seeing someone who knows he is dying, yet keeps living life to the fullest, brings us hope and a sense of peace, despite the inevitability of death.

In the last several months I have had a lot of time to reflect on, and wonder about, the role chronic illness plays in my own Christian faith. I have come to the realization that we may be misinterpreting the reasons for chronic and terminal illness.

So many of us feel like we are being punished or that our diagnosis isn't fair, but I would challenge you to reframe this life experience.

Could it be that we have been chosen? Perhaps we should feel honored and privileged. Through our attitude about, and ability to cope with our illness, we can be a model and inspiration to others, an example to help them appreciate their own blessing of health and help them grow into better people. What an extraordinary gift we can give by living honorably despite our discomfort.

If we can each strive to be a role model for others, our experience of illness will be transformed into a better and more fulfilling one, because we will discover the good that can blossom from our personal suffering.

May those of us with chronic and terminal illness strive to emulate brave people like Randy and Morrie by learning to live our lives of illness without anger, and instead delight in living the life we've been given.

My Catholic upbringing has taught me to believe that my mortality is not the end, but rather the beginning of an eternal life with God. This new life will be free from illness and suffering and will be filled with health, happiness, and love like none I can imagine. This promise of an everlasting life brings me great peace and makes the pain, trials, and sadness of my current condition more manageable.

I would like to leave you with a poem that has brought me inspiration and focus during my times of physical and mental distress.

It's In The Valleys I Grow

Sometimes life seems hard to bear,
Full of sorrow, trouble and woe
It's then I have to remember
That it's in the valleys I grow.

If I always stayed on the mountain top
And never experienced pain,
I would never appreciate God's love
And would be living in vain.

I have so much to learn
And my growth is very slow,
Sometimes I need the mountain tops,
But it's in the valleys I grow.

I do not always understand
Why things happen as they do,

But I am very sure of one thing.
My Lord will see me through.

My little valleys are nothing
When I picture Christ on the cross
He went through the valley of death;
His victory was Satan's loss.

Forgive me Lord, for complaining
When I'm feeling so very low.
Just give me a gentle reminder
That it's in the valleys I grow.

Continue to strengthen me,
Lord And use my life each day
To share your love with others
And help them find their way.

Thank you for valleys, Lord
For this one thing I know
The mountain tops are glorious
But it's in the valleys I grow!

Written by Jane Eggleston of Virginia

(John Mark Ministries, http://jmm.aaa.net.au/articles/10126.htm)

Resources

A User's Guide to Finding and Evaluating Health Information on the Web
Medical Library Association, 2003
http://www.mlanet.org/resources/userguide.html#1

American Self-Help Group Clearinghouse
http://mentalhelp.net/selfhelp/

Be an Active Member of Your Health Care Team
Food and Drug Administration, 2004
http://www.fda.gov/cder/consumerinfo/active_member.htm.
Phone: 888-463-6332

Centers for Disease Control and Prevention
National Center for Chronic Disease Prevention
and Health Promotion (NCCDPHP)
4770 Buford Hwy, NEMS K-40
Atlanta, GA 30341-3717
http://www.cdc.gov/nccdphp/

ClinicalTrials.gov
http://clinicaltrials.gov/ct/g

Cystic Fibrosis Foundation
6931 Arlington Road
Bethesda, MD 20814
www.cff.org

Five Steps to Safer Health Care
Agency for Healthcare Research and Quality, 2003
http://www.ahrq.gov/consumer/5steps.htm

Phone: 800-358-9295.

healthfinder®
Sponsored by the U.S. Department of Health and Human
Services
www.healthfinder.gov/organizations/OrgListing.asp

Health Information Resource Database
Sponsored by the National Health Information Center
www.health.gov/nhic/#Referrals

Hospice
401 Bowling Avenue, Suite 51
Nashville, TN 37205-5124
http://www.hospicenet.org

*How to Evaluate Health Information on the Internet:
Questions and Answers*
National Cancer Institute, 2003
http://cis.nci.nih.gov/fact/2_10.htm
Phone: 800-422-6237

How to Find Medical Information
National Institute of Arthritis and Musculoskeletal and Skin
Diseases, 2001
http://www.niams.nih.gov/hi/topics/howto/howto.htm
Phone: 877-226-4267

How to Get a Second Opinion
National Women's Health Information Center, 2003
http://www.4woman.gov/pub/secondopinion.htm
Phone: 800-994-WOMAN

It's in the Valleys I Grow
By Jane Eggleston

© John Mark Ministries. Articles may be reproduced in any medium, without applying for permission provided they are unedited, and retain the original author/copyright information.
http://jmm.aaa.net.au/articles/10126.htm

JAMA Patient Page: Health Information on the Internet
The Medem Network
http://www.medem.com/medlb/article_detaillb.cfm?article_ID=ZZZIJLLLTMC&sub_cat=603

MEDLINEplus®
www.nlm.nih.gov/medlineplus

National Board for Certified Counselors (NBCC)
3 Terrace Way, Suite D
Greensboro, NC 27403-3660
www.nbcc.org
Phone: 336-547-0607

National Health Information Center.
www.health.gov/nhic/pubs/tollfree.htm
Phone: 800-336-4797

National Institute of Mental Health
Public Information and Communications Branch
6001 Executive Boulevard, Room 8184, MSC 9663
Bethesda, MD 20892-9663
http://www.nimh.nih.gov/HealthInformation/GettingHelp.cfm
Phone: 866-615-6464
TTY: 301-443-8431

National Health Information Center
www.health.gov/nhic/pubs/tollfree.htm
Phone: 800-336-4797.

PubMed Central, The National Library of Medicine's
Database of Journal Articles
http://www.pubmedcentral.nih.gov/

NOAH: New York Online Access to Health.
http://www.noah-health.org/

Quick Tips – When Talking with Your Doctor
Agency for Healthcare Research and Quality, 2002
http://www.ahrq.gov/consumer/quicktips/doctalk.htm
Phone: 800-358-9295

Social Security Administration
P.O. Box 1433
Alexandria, VA 22313
www.socialsecurity.gov
Phone: 800-772-1213

Your Guide to Choosing Quality Health Care
Agency for Healthcare Research and Quality, 2002
http://www.ahrq.gov/consumer/qntool.htm
Phone: 800-358-9295

Made in the USA